Oasis 101

Poems to Spark the Imagination

Vern Alford

authorHOUSE™

1663 Liberty Drive, Suite 200
Bloomington, Indiana 47403
(800) 839-8640
www.AuthorHouse.com

First published by AuthorHouse 2/20/2006

ISBN: 1-4208-8424-7 (sc)

Printed in the United States of America
Bloomington, Indiana

This book is printed on acid-free paper.

Acknowledgement and special thanks to my
mother and greatest motivator:

JESSIE BELL BRADLEY-ALFORD 09/02/1919 - 07/03/1964
This poem was written in her honor.

LADY JESSIE BELL

Jessie Bell, my mother, oh I loved her so
She went to see The Almighty many years ago.

A lady with smarts, stamina, and pride wrapped into one;
I'm so fortunate to be one of her sons.

I remember her loving touch and accurate tongue;
She told you up front what had to be done.

Domestic work for her boss, drained much of her vitality;
But she kept focused and told us the harsh reality.

Many envied her style and quick wit;
She knew exactly what to say for your benefit.

The Jessie Bells of yesterday kept us neighborhood kids in line;
They chastised us all, told our parents, and made us mind.

I bet you know some Jessie Bells, who are still here today;
But they are a dying breed, some more will come, I pray.

For all you Jessie Bells of today, raise your kids right;
Make sure you love and guide them, they will be all right.

To all you Jessie Bells of tomorrow, today and the past;
Put your loving touch on our children so generations will last.

TABLE OF CONTENTS

Part One:
Inspirational Poems

JASMINE MEADOWS

There is a place I often go to get away and escape;
It is pleasant there and you always leave in good shape.

I love the scenery, waterfall, and jasmine flowers;
Sometimes I go there and do nothing, but sit and reflect for hours.

It's a secret place, not known by many and that's good;
For crowds often disturb nature by not doing what they should.

I'll take you there, you are special to me and I know;
You'll treasure it too, for then you'll have a special place to go.

The mind is a great adventurer and has much foresight;
Take a journey with yours sometime, it will be a pleasant flight.

Jasmine Meadows was easy to create and to me it's real;
For I often go there when my mind, body, and soul need to heal.

To find your own Jasmine Meadows, listen in silence, to your favorite
    instrumental tune;
Listen to it closely and deeply, you'll be in your own Jasmine Meadows
    real soon.

MY INSPIRATIONS

GOD created mankind to manage the earth with care;
HIS gift of birds, flowers, trees, sunlight, and rain can be seen almost
    everywhere.

Moses was chosen to free his people and was looked upon with awe;
He traveled high up on Mount Sinai to retrieve GOD'S holy law.

Ghandi was a man of great compassion, wisdom, and verve;
He challenged the British Empire with style, his will was preserved.

Martin Luther King, Jr. was a man of non- violence, human rights,
    and dreams;
His words today are often echoed and reflect many of our themes.

Mother Theresa's kind heartedness overflowed throughout distant
    lands;
With her on your side, opposition yields to her benevolent demands.

Arthur Ashe proclaimed that he was a citizen of the world and I say
    so;
He inspired many with his diplomacy, tennis, and motto.

My Grandpa Bradley was a man I loved and admired,
And he is surely responsible for many of the goals to which I aspire.

Our heroes and mentors have inspirations that motivate;
Many tried to be like them, but were unable to navigate.

If you can't find a hero to tell or show you what to do;
Just look inside yourself, you'll discover the hero in you.

FROM THE BUSH TO THE BOARDROOM

I often reflect on my African past;
Of those days in the bush and how my ancestors were cast.

Moving forward through trials and tribulations;
One cherishes each experience, despite one's frustration.

From Kings, Bushmen, or Warriors I came;
From those traditions fashioned my claim to fame.

Through the disgrace and displacement from the slave trade;
We survived the turmoil and channeled our rage.

Inspite of family separation, our bond was still strong;
For we had the inner strength to carry on.

We helped build this nation, but got no recognition.
For our hard work and determination are African traditions.

Within our church where many learned men first read;
We honed our values for others to spread.

Sharecropping and Southern living taught me well,
How to conquer the Urban blight, where some others fell.

Our schools were believed inferior, at least that's what they say;
But it prepared us for the many hardships along the way.

Through each obstacle you learn what is true;
For conflict and struggle help ensure the strength in you.

Now as a leader I recognize this scheme;
That our lives go full circle through THE ALMIGHTY'S DREAM.

FOUR WAYS

Thunder, lightening, the sun, and rain
Provide energy and nourishment so the earth is sustained.

Character, trust, harmony, and prayer
Inspire one to achieve genuineness everywhere.

Family, friends, teachers, and leaders;
Help to nurture the resolve of their believers.

Hawks, eagles, bats, and owls, those birds of prey;
Find contentment capturing their bounty, two by night, two by day.

Drugs, anger, violence, and war are things many of us explore;
But laughter, friendship, peace, and heaven's euphoria, satisfy us
    more.

Stress, paranoia, envy, and rage
Often prematurely lead you to your grave.

Racism, bigotry, hatred, and sin;
These frequent behaviors make it difficult for us to be friends.

For love, happiness, unity, and respect;
Will pull us together to conquer neglect.

The things we see, hear, feel, and say;
Should be motivators leading us to pray.

A SPECIAL PERSON

There was a special person born some time ago;
Whose arrival would change the world we know.

He was born of special parents who knew His goal;
For His would be the greatest story ever told.

The life He lived enlightened us each day;
For He taught us how to love, believe, and pray.

The miracles He performed throughout His years
Bring joy to my heart and fill my eyes with tears.

Many doubted and taunted Him, for that He paid a price;
For on the cross He died for us, the ultimate sacrifice.

His worldly existence was not without reason;
He is truly, truly the beacon of every season.

I keep Him secure and safe in my heart;
For I need His wisdom and guidance, The Almighty is so smart.

Yes, Jesus Christ, the Son of GOD and Father of man;
Has promised us everlasting life through the ALMIGHTY'S hand.

Vern Alford

JESUS WAS A LIBERAL

The religious right claim to know the Bible best;
But I want to tell you about Jesus, so you'll know the rest.

Born of the Virgin Mary, that should be your first clue;
For He was a special person, not born a Gentile, but a Jew.

All the religious elders in the temple soon realized
That this kid Jesus had different words of wisdom, much to their
   surprise.

He befriended Mary Magdalene, maybe a woman of ill repute;
That didn't bother Him, for the dirtier the soul, the greater His
   pursuit.

Among the common folk He was loved and respected;
But Cesar's army hunted and wanted Him collected.

He fed the 5 thousand with just two fish and five loaves of bread;
Try doing that today, you'll go out of your head.

Some of us think, we are better than most;
But, you recipients of that perceived gift need not boast.

So, conservatives, liberals and all the rest;
You'll all be the same, when you take your creator's test.

Today is as good a day as any to make that change;
Reach out to your brothers and sisters, then GOD's likeness you can
   begin to proclaim

UNIFICATION

There are many different races throughout the earth's vast land;
We spend much time fighting each other, for what, I don't
understand.

I have read of many people who tried to unite us as one,
They seem to rapidly disappear before their job is done.

I wonder about my descendants and what they will find,
If we do not fix this world before we run out of time.

There has to be a solution to these problems we face,
Let us cherish each other's identity, like we do our own namesake.

One often dream about tomorrow and all the riches it might bring,
But others dread the possible destruction of everything.

Man has become so smart that he can make himself extinct,
But he has not realized that his transmitters could be on the brink.

I'm hopeful that we will find peace in this world one day,
Let us begin by listening to what others have to say.

By fixing what we can today, tomorrow should be grand;
Life is so great, especially when we walk hand in hand.

JUST PASSING THROUGH

I'm just passing through this world, I only have a minute;
I'm glad I ran upon you and grateful this world has you in it.

I'm just passing through this world, there is lots to enjoy;
Like watching a video game of a girl being locked onto by a boy.

I'm just passing through this world, but was able to get a glance;
Of your beautiful face and our silhouette during our romance.

I'm just passing through this world enroute to the universe;
I really enjoyed the spontaneity, we did not need to rehearse.

I'm just passing through this world, I hope I touched your heart;
For love often comes easier to those who had a genuine part.

I'm just passing through this world and it needs help from you;
So, consider leaving something special behind to help see the project
     through.

I'm just passing through this world and one day my journey will end;
It's good that we met and I believe our paths will cross again.

I PRAYED FOR YOU

I prayed for you before I knew;
I prayed for you because I knew you would be true.

I prayed for you to make my life fulfilled;
I prayed for you through my beaming internal will.

I prayed for you to match my zest for life;
I prayed for you so that our love would not be sacrificed.

I prayed for you so we could share;
I prayed for our love to be hailed every where.

I prayed for you to fulfill my needs;
I prayed so hard and long, you would not believe.

I will pray for you after I am gone;
I will pray for you to have the strength to carry on.

I will pray for you when we both join again;
Then we will pray together, for others, before they begin.

BUTTERFLIES OF SPRING

In a cocoon just waiting to get herself complete;
To enter this world as something cute and unique.

Spread your wings and break free of your cage;
For nothing can contain you, you have a world to amaze.

The colors of the rainbow and more are you;
Of course Heaven made you, you are so cute, too.

The elegance of your style, flow and grace;
Are reinforced when you fly or float any place.

Flowers and children's hands are resting places you enjoy;
It doesn't matter if you are held by a girl or a boy.

I've captured butterflies before, but quickly let them go free;
For I soon realized that I wouldn't want anyone to do that to me.

Not to be captured and kept as a pet;
For you, flying so carefree is the best sight yet.

The essence of springtime and its ever changing season
Helps us love you more, we have good reason.

We all like springtime, it's the most beautiful time of year;
It escorts you in, I'm glad it brought you here.

The butterfly, the symbol of freedom, beauty, and grace
Brightens onlookers, leaving a smile on their face.

The butterflies of spring, only here for a short time;
Will return next year; again, everything will be fine.

HAVE YOU EVER

Have you ever wished upon a star?
And rediscovered your love from afar.

Have you ever laid on a sunny beach?
And felt the ocean's water rushing between your toes and feet.

Have you ever had a taste for something sweet?
Then remembered that your lover's kiss could not be beat.

Have you ever been in pain beyond belief?
Then felt the loving that brought you relief.

Have you ever chased a butterfly as a child?
Then sat and marveled at its beauty for awhile.

Have you ever praised GOD for all the gifts given you?
And yearned to share those gifts with others too.

Have you ever wanted to be touched and held real tight?
Which made you believe everything was alright.

Have you ever felt loneliness and wondered why?
Just to remember you just told your lover goodbye.

Have you ever felt awkward or confused?
And the funny joke you just heard made you amused.

Have you ever gone on a date just to find?
That the one you were with wasn't on your mind.

Have you ever been alone in a crowd of friends?
And wondered when you would see your lover again.

13

Have you ever settled for something just to be nice?
And later regretted making that sacrifice.

Have you ever felt at peace among confusion?
To realize your lover had prevented any intrusion.

Have you ever lost your comfort zone?
Just to find out you were not alone.

Have you ever tried something risky?
And remembered that kiss which made you frisky.

Have you ever been brave in a moment of fear?
To find out it was your resolve in that single little tear.

Have you ever been pursued by someone from your past?
And that pursuit made you feel good, you wanted it to last.

Have you ever felt so good you couldn't believe it to be true?
For you just recently realized that someone special loves you.

Have you ever anticipated the future and all it could bring?
Knowing all along that you only wanted one thing.

Have you ever felt complete and praised the ONE above?
For reconnecting you with the one you really love.

GIVE GOD A HIGH FIVE

Who gave your parents the ability to conceive?
Look at you now, all delivered and able to breathe.

Growing up through the years with many trials and tribulations;
Your parents put you in GOD'S hands to handle many situations.

On your own now, you still backslide and sometimes go astray;
GOD has a plan for you, you'll get back on track one day.

Treat yourself and others with respect and always be true;
Others will like you for who you are, there is really nothing else to
    do.

Achieve all you can in life, but keep GOD close around;
During desperate and good times HE can always be found.

You are in HIS image, so be a good role model in life;
For if you get to the hereafter, you'll be that role model twice.

None have been to heaven and back, as near as I can tell;
But you must decide to live right or you'll create your own living hell.

We all have choices, GOD gave us that right;
But what you decide to do with yours, you'll live with, day and night.

When you make it through and you are ready to plant your own seed;
You'll be ready for parenthood where you can continue the good
    deed.

JASPER JONES

Jasper Jones was a poor ole soul;
But he had something more precious than gold.

Very frail and really up there in years;
He had so much knowledge to ease your fears.

An old run down shack on the poor side of town;
Where folk needing advice seemed to always hang around.

Didn't talk much, but really listened to you;
Then he would mostly say, you know what to do.

Need confirmation, talk to Jasper Jones, bend his ear;
What little he told you made things very clear.

Jasper went to glory some years ago;
I still reminisce his remarks, I miss him so.

Much of Jasper Jones lives on in me til today;
When in a fix, I'd think, what would Jasper say.

BEYOND CRISIS

I'm in crisis each day of my life;
As my conscience avoids man's imposed paradise.

Born with a choice to fight life's scheming temptations;
Choose your battles wisely and know their locations.

Obstacles prepare you for passage beyond transition;
Life is a cycle of change manifested in the simplest condition.

Bombarded with news so sad and distressing;
We still seek it out, that's even more depressing.

Those who are angry, uptight, and burdened with stress;
Consider this antidote - focus on the positives, you'll worry less.

Managed crisis shapes your future and modifies your goal;
So, be one with the energy that chose your soul.

MY BLACK PEARL

Traveling throughout this vast and complex world;
I have never come upon one, beyond you, my black pearl.

A face so hot and mellow it glows upon sight,
She impresses you with her smile during the day and moonlight.

A proportionate body, so well defined and nice;
I want to be next to it, regardless of the sacrifice.

When she speaks, her lips protrude with a sexy smile;
It puts you in a trance, mesmerizing you for a while.

Her walk and that talk, such things of class;
Make me stare at her, especially at that cute round ass.

My black pearl is beautiful, smart, wise and sweet;
I am so fascinated with her everyday of the week.

My black pearl gives me power, fortune and pride;
I know she's down with me, that she cannot hide.

Many don't have a black pearl to boast about each day;
But if you find one, keep her near and listen to what she has to say.

Most men never find a black pearl to cherish and love;
But if you ever get one, be thankful to the One above.

Make sure not to take her for granted and always be true;
Others are waiting for the chance to lure her from you.

So, to you my black pearl, remember this phrase;
You'll bring joy to me, I hope, throughout all my days.

Now that I have my black pearl, my life is complete;
I really enjoy being with her, especially between the sheets.

TRANSITION

I thought I failed until I met you;
Life was bleak, but now it's not so blue.

In times of distress and despair, one should not be alone;
Knowing and being with you has brought me happiness I have never
known.

Life is short, or so I thought during moments of desperation;
But, life is long through you and I fight to avoid the separation.

Man has loved, man has lived, throughout the ages;
This man has been blessed with your love, as he has become more brave
and courageous.

Life is a host of transitions we should anticipate;
Meet each one head on, then you'll be able to navigate.

OVER THE HORIZON

Over the horizon, where I long to be;
All those beautiful things just waiting there for me.
Here, where I am, not satisfied;
For over the horizon, I believe, is my greatest prize.

Over the horizon, we all look and want for much more;
Sometimes though, those treasures aren't what we looked for.
Take life as it comes, there is room for modification;
Over the horizon just might be too much anticipation.

Over the horizon, we have searched for years without stop;
We think once there, we're at the top.
Life is good, don't let it pass you by too soon;
For over the horizon, sometimes unhappiness looms.

Over the horizon, of many a dream and aspiration;
Eagerly seeking that destination with much expectation.
One should have dreams, keep them within reason;
Over the horizon, things change too, as do the season.

Over the horizon, that pursuit, sometime just let it go;
Reflect on it later, then there is so much more to know.
As days pass our knowledge becomes more refined;
Then toward those over the horizon goals, you'll be more inclined.

Over the horizon preoccupation, many have that notion, as do I;
Just remember, don't loose sight here, give earth a try.
Life's development gives you many things to achieve;
That over the horizon desire is but one of these.

Over the horizon dreamers, there are many of us out there;
Choose your goals wisely, we're all going somewhere.
I dare you to dream, plan and explore;
Over the horizon is just a dream too, one you can make much more.

21

WHEN I LAUGH

When I laugh I feel so complete;
Oh, so much joy from my head to feet.

I love to laugh, a time to relax and have fun;
A time to be myself for real, as though time has just begun.

The sound of laughter comes in all expressions and styles;
I just love to see and hear it, don't you, people relaxing with their
     smiles.

When my laughter comes, I can't control the sound;
For I laugh hard and deeply, people hear it all around.

Real laughter is something you can't ever delay;
Sometimes it appears unexpectedly, just passing your way.

Laughter is healthy, I believe it cleanses the soul;
It engulfs your whole body when its you it beholds.

Laughter is rich with pride and so carefree;
As it touches you it decides when to let you be.

When I laugh, there is nothing as joyous as that time;
Where I can express my emotions, knowing everything is fine.

When I laugh I experience the great sounds of joy, once trapped
     inside;
Radiating from my vocals, now there is nowhere to hide.

I enjoy laughter, I hope you do as well;
I find laughter everyday, sometimes in stories others tell.

Don't spend a day without laughter, find it somewhere;
Once you unleash your laughter, problems are easier to bear.

Look for laughter in many things in life, its good to let go;
For pent up frustrations and anger have nothing good to show.

KING COBRA, KING COBRA

King Cobra, King Cobra, you have intrigued us for years and do til
    this day;
I'm not a betting man, but I bet your mystery will stay.
From ancient Egypt where you graced Kings and Queens;
A major part of any ritual or celebration always put you at the scene.

King Cobra, King Cobra, great source of income for snake charmers;
The myth is the King Cobra is brutal, but they are not only harmers.
Can expand their neck which looks very intimidating;
But they are just posturing their physique, some say anticipating.

King Cobra, King Cobra, I wonder how you remain the boss;
With all your competitors trying to topple you, it's surely their loss.
You have the title, you were rightfully named for we all agree;
Your style, character, elegance and grace are exactly what a king should
    be.

King Cobra, King Cobra, I just love to see you dance;
You seem to do it deliberately, putting us in a trance.
Rather than fight you'll gracefully flee the scene;
But once provoked, you strike quickly, deadly and clean.

King Cobra, King Cobra, your numbers decreasing, not yet extinct;
You should be in protective custody, its later than you think.
Your charm, pride and strength are great attributes for sure;
Others would like to be like you, but were unable to endure.

Part Two:
Romantic Poems

THE FLOWER IN YOUR RAINBOW

I saw a bud in the mist of the morning dew;
As that bud blossomed, I knew that flower was you.

Flowers radiate from warmth, moisture, and serenity of the air;
As do your lips, while readying for my pair.

The flower, the bud, is the essence of you;
Its shape and curves electrify me through and through.

The rainbow that traveled so radiantly across the skies
Is reflected and protected in your big beautiful eyes.

With all its colors, sharpness, and contrast;
Such a sight to see, one I hope will always last.

Rainbows will never be the same to me anymore;
For each rainbow I see now will remind me of the one I adore.

Things in nature are exquisitely defined;
And I cherish the thought of you being mine.

SIMPLY BECAUSE YOU ARE YOU

I like your honesty, humor, and nerve;
You really know how to counter opposition, side step an approaching
curve.

I like your loyalty, tenderness, and eagerness to explore;
For you have embarked on an expedition that will land you at my
door.

I like your commitment, posture, and I seldom see tears;
Cause you have many means of handling conflicts, and easing one's
fears.

I like the lust in your eyes as you discern an intimate desire;
You know I'm willing to participate, by doing what you require.

I like your distinctive cheeks, suggestive lips, and the palm of your
hand;
Cause when our hands are joined together they convey my desire to be
your man.

When asked a question you respond with thought and lots of insight;
One does not doubt your resolve for you are consistently right.

I like to hear you laugh when amused, as you are then carefree;
For during these times I like to believe you are closer to me.

I like how you invoke, in common folk, the need to be genuine and
smart;
You maneuver others toward a certain goal, truly a work of art.

I like to feel that you are my friend in whom I can confide;
Who redirects my frustration and still respects my pride.

These thoughts inherent in you are my true convictions,
Cause I believe you need to be exalted for preserving a vanishing
tradition.

So, if during times of opposing forces one generally questions your
nerve;
Just remember, those who are authentic generally get what they
deserve.

WHEN I LOOK AT YOU

When I look at you, I see the radiant fire
That ignites the flame of my burning desire.

When I look at you, I fall on my knees to gently pray
For the hope of our connection before time slips away.

When I look at you, I see the genuiness of your heart and soul;
For I believed our destiny would be revealed since I was about twelve
    years old.

When I look at you, I'm compelled to fantasize and dream
Of all those thrilling liaisons that cause our hearts to beam.

When I look at you, I often stop, ponder and stare;
Being amongst your beauty, more refreshing than a breath of mountain's
    fresh air.

When I look at you, I see the calmness of the Pacific Ocean;
Your calmness has afflicted me with your awesome love potion.

When I look at you, I see the concern of a true friend;
Who acknowledges my worth and lets me lean on her again and
    again.

When I look at you, I see the happiness in your eyes;
I know to follow you throughout our journey, you are my chosen
    guide.

When I look at you, I see the beauty that exists;
I try to contain myself, but sometimes I can't resist.

When I look at you, I am able to end this day in style;
For I know I'll see you tomorrow, which makes waiting worthwhile.

Yes, I have looked at you all these days;
I plan to look at you forever, Lord let me ride this wave.

Vern Alford

LOVING YOU

I've loved for a long time but would not say
How I felt and that the feeling grew stronger each day.

Some men keep certain secrets buried deep inside;
Oftentimes not revealing them, cause to us, we looked jive.

I regret not expressing these feelings before;
But I was not willing to risk being rejected once more.

For some reason I took the risk and did finally express
The joy you bring by filling my life with happiness.

I learned a great lesson through this little skit;
That saying "I LOVE YOU" did not hurt even a little bit.

There is a confession to be made about my appetite for your love;
For I long to caress your inner loins til you soar like a dove.

All the passion I feel can not be contained;
So come get the love beast, hold onto his reigns.

I thought I was tamed until I smelled you my sweet;
Now your scent gets me so excited I can't stay in my seat.

So, I leave you now with this simple phrase and thought;
That the fiery love you'll get from me hasn't even been taught.

JUST SWINGING

Soaring on the park swing amidst the summer's breeze
Should bring euphoria as you sky among the trees;

He pushed you higher and then the swing began to buckle;
She screamed with excitement, but he just laughed and chuckled.

Overlooking the parkway, city lights, and the river's curve;
Gives you fantasies to ponder about things over yonder, if you got the
    nerve.

Now you have the eagle's eye, so use that treasured gift;
To hone the love fibers of that man whose push was so swift.

As you soar tomorrow toward your majestic height;
Just remember, he who pushed you once, still has you in his sight.

PRECIOUS MOMENTS

Precious moments are those spent with you each day;
Precious moments are the intimate thoughts I beam your way.

A precious moment is gazing at your lucious lips;
Hoping to soon kiss and caress them and your gentle fingertips.

A precious moment is perceiving your exotic will and delight;
For the love you get from me will suit you just right.

A precious moment is knowing we're inseparable in every way;
And being able to harbor that bond in love, work and play.

Precious moments are evident every time we embrace;
For those are the frequent times I yearn to be in your space.

Precious moments are those realistic goals that we made
About our future and how that ground work was laid.

A precious moment is walking with you on a sunny beach
And later playing roller derby, together, between the black satin
    sheets.

A precious moment is how you notice me in a passing glance
For that quick gaze starts my nature to love dance.

Yes, those precious moments with you I'll cherish for eternity;
And being with you forever helps to maintain my serenity.

HUNGRY FOR YOU BABY

I am so hungry for you baby that my heart skips a beat,
Then marches double time so there is no repeat.

I am so hungry for you baby, a cosmic minute of the universe pauses
    to proclaim
That my passionate love for you has been heavenly sustained.

I am so hungry for you baby, I need no majestic persuasion;
I just need your love which satisfies all occasions.

I am so hungry for you baby, no fantasy is ever complete;
So I savor that moment of us being sweaty under the sheet.

SLEEPLESS NIGHTS

Last night I fell asleep, but you weren't in my bed
It took forever to get forty winks because my hunger was not fed.

I need your tender loving to satify this thirsty soul;
It gets its nourishment from you - cause I fit your mold.

I'll try to sleep again tonight, but where will you be?
I know I'll sleep much better if you sleep with me.

HOT PURSUIT

I want to enter your anatomical chamber to see
Whether that cunning adventure is really meant for me.

That maiden voyage would certainly be thrilling;
And for repeat expeditions I am definitely willing.

Unlike the Player who only see women as his prey;
I prefer to be gentle and tender, loving you day after day.

The goals one sets are to be pursued;
My goal is you, so our omph can be renewed.

So I leave you now, but keep this thought;
That our desire for each other has been mutually sought.

I'M NOT AVAILABLE

I'm not available, I'm poised to tell the world
That I've found someone special to me, more precious than any pearl.

I'm not available and I like saying that line;
When another had me, she played me, now she ran out of time.

I'm not available and it feels so damn good;
I'd never thought I could feel this way, I feel like a lover should.

I'm not available, that phrase cuts searchers down to size;
I proudly wear that banner on my chest so others recognize.

I'm not available, one already caught my eye;
And when it happened, I did not need to ask why.

I'm not available and I treasure the thought
Of knowing this love of mine only goes to the one I sought.

I'm not available and now I am a brand new me;
I will give you more love than you have ever known, just you wait and
    see.

I'm not available everybody, now listen to this tip;
When the right one comes along, a man is glad to be whipped.

NEVER GIVE UP ON LOVE

Never give up on love, it will come one day;
And when it arrives, grab it, don't you delay.

Love is always lurking somewhere, out there among us;
Sometimes its very quiet, sometimes it makes a fuss.

It comes at you in many disguises, you might not have a clue
That love tapped you on the shoulder, leaving you to wonder what to
    do..

Don't fight that feeling many can't describe;
But love can catch you off guard, what a big surprise.

When you say "I LOVE YOU", those words are so intense;
But, until its reciprocated your heart is deep in suspense.

When its mutual your joys are outtasight;
If it's false or make believe, you get very uptight.

Test the love jones by feeling it through your heart and soul;
It will guide you all the way, for a lie it never told.

Many think they are in love because of looks and conditions;
Don't fall for that window dressing, when it's real you'll take notice
    and listen.

Those of us fortunate enough to have love nicely tucked away;
Are readily distinguishable by the behavior we display.

Those out there without love, just be poised;
For love will come to you too, but might not make any noise.

Vern Alford

Love has its own timetable and there are no rules;
But when love comes to you, it knew who to choose.

Be patient, my friends, for life goes on tomorrow;
And then when love comes, you'll have no more sorrow.

HEART AND SOUL

I lost my genuineness chasing my professional dream;
During that time I was rude, selfish, competitive, and mean.

Once on top I still longed to belong;
But found no peace until you came along.

Man seems compelled to conquer, control, and to have power;
But what he really wants and needs is you, a precious flower.

So, during our twilight years we often confess;
Of wanting true happiness in life and no more emptiness.

No more reaching for the stars at your expense;
I now reach for you because you are my heart's content.

MY ALPHABET FOR YOU

"A" is for **always**, which is when I think of you.
"B" is for the **beauty** you possess that is so true.

"C" is for the **charming** charisma that exists,
"D" is for the **deliciousness** and tenderness of your kiss.

"E" is for the **everlasting** feelings we share;
"F" is for the **friendship** that will never despair.

"G" is for the **grace** in you, that all see so clear;
"H" is for the **happiness** you bring that causes me to cheer.

"I" is for the **intimacy** I feel when we are alone;
"J" is for the **jasmine** fragrance that lingers wherever you roam.

"K" is for the **kindness** that you have inside;
"L" is for the **love** I have for you that I wear with pride.

"M" is for the **magic** that I feel in my heart;
"N" is for the **nourishment** I hope will never depart.

"O" is for the **openness** that we share always;
"P" is for the **passion** I will have for you throughout all my days.

"Q" is for the **quenching** refreshment of your kiss;
"R" is for the **radiance** of your smile and its freshness.

"S" is for the **sexiness** of your walk;
"T" is for the **tenderness** of your speech when you talk.

"U" is for the **undeniable** love and respect your energy demands;
"V" is for the **velocity** of my heartbeat when felt by your hand
.

"W" is for the **wisdom** you use to offset intrusion;
"X" is for the **xylose** you use to sweeten any solution.

"Y" is for **yesterday** and the emptiness of the hour;
"Z" is for the **zest** and gusto that springs from you, my flower.

My **alphabet** for you is clear you see;
All of them describe some of the essence of thee.

EAGLE MEETS THE DOVE

Soaring high in the skies above,
The eagle sights the poised and majestic dove.

Gliding down for a closer view,
The dove and eagle's eyes met, they both knew.

Soaring again, the eagle climbed to his greatest height;
He was hoping to impress the dove with all his might.

Strutting around on the earth's floor
The dove waited for the eagle to end his courting soar.

The eagle came down to take another glance
And joined the dove, now both are sitting on an olive branch.

Their courtship began, what a joyous display;
For the eagle mounted the dove, day after day.

The two had captured a time and needed to explore;
How their relationship would be forever more.

An eagle and a dove, what an unlikely pair;
Would spread the joy of their union, everywhere.

So, to all the eagles who will soar the skies to find;
Observe the one noticing you, she might be your kind.

The eagle and dove flew away to nest;
And, of course, their relationship developed into the best.

One still see them around from time to time;
If you wonder how they are doing, they are doing just fine.

AN ANGEL ON HOLIDAY

An angel on holiday came forth for a tour;
When I first spotted her, I then began my lure.

I thought I wouldn't get far, but had to risk
The opportunity of a lifetime or just, later, reminisce.

Within her view I stood so proud and tall;
I left nothing to chance, I gave it my all.

She glanced my way and then inquired;
Whether I was standing there to be admired.

Too embarrassed to speak, I just swallowed my pride;
Then she said, take my hand, I'll be your guide.

At that moment I was instantly transformed and made anew;
Then I vowed to do anything she asked me to.

While I'm here, she said, will you spend some time
Showing me your life, if you are not in a bind?

So engulfed in her, I became selfish and asked;
How long will your tour down here last?

I must return soon, I want to stay here with you;
But duty calls and I have chores to do.

I refuse to let you go, I thought in my mind;
So I got on my knees and asked GOD for more time.

Take as long as you need, but know this my son;
Treat her like gold so you both can become one.

My angel is still here, happy and full of life;
You see, GOD delivers, you don't have to ask twice.

So, as we plan our future, I am still amazed;
That an angel on holiday, came here and stayed.

LOOKING THROUGH

Looking through my focused eyes;
I see the silhoutte of my future bride.

I look beyond the image to glance
Whether that image has, again, put me in a trance.

I don't mind being consumed by you;
For you have already fulfilled me, through and through.

I realize now that we all go through phases;
But baby, you send me through sensual stages.

The very thought of you, brings me exhilaration and thrill;
For you are like fine wine when slightly chilled.

I nourish on you to feed and satisfy my soul;
You know baby, you really taught me how to rock "n" roll.

I will surely go on because I now believe;
That our ultimate liaison will, most definitely, be achieved.

So I leave you now with this simple phrase;
I'll love you forever and throughout all my days.

LUSCIOUS LIPS

I found a pair of luscious lips, they were on your face.
I found a pair of luscious lips, whose imprint could not be erased.

I found a pair of luscious lips, just waiting for me to kiss.
I found a pair of luscious lips, that looked so inviting, I could not resist.

I found a pair of luscious lips; slightly opened and tongue exposed.
I found a pair of luscious lips; waiting to be consoled.

I found a pair of luscious lips, so juicy, full of life, and deep red.
I found a pair of luscious lips, whose sight sent me out of my head.

I found a pair of luscious lips, more beautiful than you'll ever know.
I found a pair of luscious lips, that complimented your face so.

I found a pair of luscious lips, just waiting to be pleased.
I found a pair of luscious lips, that was my greatest tease.

I found a pair of luscious lips, I just had to kiss and touch.
I found a pair of luscious lips, that caressed my hungry lips so very much.

I found a pair of luscious lips, and this I can not describe.
I found a pair of luscious lips, that made my nature really come alive.

I now have that pair of luscious lips, combined on my lips you see.
I'll forever have these luscious lips to kiss and pleasure me.

FINDERS KEEPERS

Wasn't looking for anyone then you came by;
Your radiant light, glowing with sunshine, caught my eye.

Among life's creations I wondered if there was one for me;
I thought my journey was in twilight then you came before me.

Age is a number some use to decide how to live;
Ignore those hang-ups you learned before, take what I have to give.

I know from experience that joy is sweet and, oh, so nice;
Don't go through life alone, be careful when you roll the dice.

A test of your will should show you the path;
Take the road of pleasure, those benefits might last.

As you make your decision of who will be your mate;
Don't spend too much time wondering, then you'll make a mistake.

If you choose me, I will forever quench your thirst;
I recognized your beauty before you did, I saw your inside first.

Go with your gut and release your spunky, inner child;
For it got you here, it will carry you on with style.

So I leave you now with this simple task;
Choose a man who loves you, for that relationship will last.

LOOK INSIDE MY HEART

Look inside my heart to know and experience the real me;
Look closer and deeper; I know you'll like what you see.

Its chamber is strong and beats loudly like a drum;
Listen to its rhythm, never a ho hum.

That old pain in my heart has faded into the past;
For the joy I know of you is sure to last.

The hope and belief you see, developed from frustration and despair;
All I need from you is a glance or stare to take me anywhere.

You took me to a height I'd never known or seen before;
As long as I am with you I'll peak there forever more.

I looked inside my heart the other day and saw all its joy and pride;
I saw you in my heart's main chamber, we were standing side by side.

What others see inside your heart is a reflection of you;
As they come to know your goodness they will want to be in there
    too.

UNCONDITIONAL LOVE

I love you for one reason and thats because I do;
I do not need any special consideration, I just need and want you.

It's not just because you are sexy and oh so sweet;
It's not just because you are smart and in books, you can't be beat.

It's not just because you tolerate me and accept my advances;
It's not just because you let me come back and give me second
   chances.

I love you unconditionally and that love is true.
I need no special consideration, I just want to be around you.
Yes, I love you unconditionally and that love is true;
I need no special consideration, all I need is you.

It's not just because you are beautiful, charming and just plain nice;
It's because I do, I don't need to think twice.

It's not just because you are funny, quick and very wise;
It's because you make me feel special which keeps me beaming with
   pride.

It's not just because you are classy, honest and a cut above;
It's because you captured my heart, you made me fall in love.

I love you unconditionally and that love is true;
I need no special consideration, I just want to be around you.
Yes, I love you unconditionally and that love is true;
I need no special consideration, all I need is you.

It's not just because of your walk, smile or luscious lips;
It's not just because of your temperment, poise or shapely hips.

It's not just because of your style, charm and grace;
It's not just because you turn heads when you walk into any place.

It's not just because you are curious, open and have common sense;
It's not just because you are friendly, wise and never seen tense.

I love you unconditionally and that love is true;
I need no special consideration, I just want to be around you.
Yes, I love you unconditionally and that love is true;
I need no special consideration, all I need is you.

It's not just because you look inside me with those big cute eyes;
But your desire to be around me is such a pleasant surprise.
I can't resist the thought of being around you, maybe you have me
    hypnotized.

Yes, I love you unconditionally and not because of your perks;
I love you for who you are and thats why this relationship works.
I love you unconditionally and that love is true.
I need no special consideration, all I need is you.

I'M SATISFIED, SATISFIED

As I learned to walk, and later began to talk;
I'm satisfied, satisfied.

When it became loose, I pulled my first tooth;
I'm satisfied, satisfied.

When I learned to ride a bike, as a small tyke;
I'm satisfied, satisfied.

Doing good in school, learning the golden rule;
I'm satisfied, satisfied.

As an invincible teen, there were many things I had never seen;
I'm satisfied, satisfied.

My first love rendezvous, with someone so true;
I'm satisfied, satisfied.

Off to college, to get more knowledge;
I'm satisfied, satisfied.

A good job came fast, and my employment last;
I'm satisfied, satisfied.

Traveling across this vast land, I finally realized the master plan;
I'm satisfied, satisfied.

I finally got you, the one I love so true;
I'm satisfied, satisfied.

Life is a journey we take in stride, always keep your head up and walk
    with pride;
I'm satisfied, so satisfied.

Vern Alford

GOOD MORNING MY LOVE

Good morning my love, as always, I'm thinking of you;
You are trapped inside my heart, there is nothing you can do.

Good morning my love, life should be good to us;
We have mastered the art of being with the one we trust.

Good morning my love, it's another beautiful day;
Make sure you enjoy yourself in work, love, and play.

Good morning my love, each day you are blessed;
Knowing I am right here beside you and I love you best.

Good morning my love, dream of me inside you tonight;
For there will come a time again for us, everything will be alright.

Good morning my love, I will say that to you forever and a day;
For I love you so deeply you see, YES, it will always be that way.

Good morning my love, I just love to say that to you;
Each time I say those words, you seem to be so fascinated too.

Good morning my love, the joy of my life is you with me forever;
I'll always be with you, there is nothing to worry about, ever.

A ROSE ON YOUR PILLOW

I put a rose on your pillow to get your undivided attention;
There are somethings I need to say, somethings I must mention.

I'm not good with words, but wanted you to know;
That I am really blessed to be loved by you so.

I am not perfect, but this I pledge right now;
That I'll be the best man you can imagine, someway, somehow.

I'll be there for you through trials and tribulations;
I'll be there during times of happiness and shower you with flirtations.

You make me feel complete and I must return the favor;
Baby, you please me in so many ways, I just love your frisky behavior.

The way you laugh, with all that energy and sexiness of the sound;
Keeps me saying things amusing to you, you are great to be around.

The way you talk, the sexiness of your voice;
Drives me insane over you baby, I have no other choice.

The way we make love is so amazing, none can compare;
You satisfy me so much, my excitement sprinkles everywhere.

I want to satisfy your needs in each and every way;
I want to be your best buddy always, that will make my day.

You deserve to be recognized and I'll gladly tell the world;
That you are the best thing that ever happened to me, you are my girl.

So with this rose, enjoy its meaning, beauty and intent;
For I want you to realize that you are the "BEST", heaven ever sent.

TELL HER YOU LOVE HER

Tell her you love her, that will make her feel secure;
Tell her you love her, but only if you are sure.

Tell her you love her and just wait awhile;
Tell her you love her, watch that beaming bright smile.

Tell her you love her and that everything is ok;
Tell her you love her and that it will always be that way.

Tell her you love her, say it out loud;
Tell her you love her, that will make her so proud.

Tell her you love her, look her in the eyes;
Tell her you love her, kiss her, and wait for those sighs.

Tell her you love her, never play with her feelings;
Tell her you love her, a happy heart never needs healing.

Tell her you love her, each and everyday;
Tell her you love her, she'll be thrilled to hear you say.

Tell her you love her, and take my advice;
Tell her you love her, that will make her feel so nice.

Tell her you love her and show the world;
Tell her you love her and she will always be your girl.

Tell her you love her, those words have such awesome power;
Tell her you love her, hour, after hour, after hour.

Tell her you love her, say it soft and mild;
Tell her you love her, she might bear your child.

Tell her you love as soon as you are awake;
Tell her you love her at night, for heavens sake.

A LADY WANTS A GENTLEMAN

A lady wants a gentleman who is sensitive, secure, and wise;
A lady wants a gentleman who has a beaming positive drive.
But a woman just wants a man.

A lady wants a gentleman who is charming, clever, and a little bold;
A lady wants a gentleman who knows how and when to take control.
But a woman just wants a man.

A lady wants a gentleman who is never timid and takes a stand;
A lady wants a gentleman who is no push-over, he'll do all he can.
But a woman just wants a man.

A lady wants a gentleman who can be bashful when the time is right;
A lady wants a gentleman who is comforting to her at night.
But a woman just wants a man.

A lady wants a gentleman who is highly regarded by his peers;
A lady wants a gentleman who will be content with her throughout
    their years.
But a woman just wants a man.

A lady wants a gentleman who is his own leader, by choice;
A lady wants a gentleman who appropriately responds to her calm
    voice.
But a woman just wants a man.

A lady wants a gentleman who has goals, ideas, and dreams;
A lady wants a gentleman who takes those steps with her as a team.
But a woman just wants a man.

A lady wants a gentleman who appreciates her emotions and feelings;
A lady wants a gentleman who is to her, strong and revealing.
But a woman just wants a man.

A lady wants a gentleman who is dependable, trustworthy, and has
    class;
A lady wants a gentleman who assures her that their love will last.
But a woman just wants a man.

A lady wants a gentleman who has family values and a sense of duty;
A lady wants a gentleman who shows that he loves her truly.
But a woman just wants a man.

A lady wants a gentleman who is distinguished and sound;
A lady wants a gentleman who, with her, can be a clown.
But a woman just wants a man.

A lady wants a gentleman who pampers her and is, oh, so smooth;
A lady wants a gentleman who, with her, knows when to be cool.
But a woman just wants a man.

A lady wants a gentleman who is genuine and sweet;
A lady wants a gentleman who will caress her from her head to feet.
But a woman just wants a man.

A lady wants a gentleman who listens to what she has to say;
A lady wants a gentleman who responds to her in a kind and genuine
    way.
But a woman just wants a man.

A lady wants a gentleman who will satisfy her every need;
A lady wants a gentleman who she, can only please.
But a woman just wants aman.

All these qualities that a lady desires are top shelf;
That lady should be poised to get that gentleman for herself.
But the woman will simply settle for somebody else.

Vern Alford

THE LADY'S ELEGANCE

A lady's elegance is often seen;
By a man's fascination when he appears on the scene.

A lady's elegance is always unique and sweet;
It uprights onlookers and knocks them off their feet.

A lady's elegance gives a man unlimited and uncharted powers;
His attraction for her lasts and lingers for hours.

A lady's elegance disarms those who are rude, angry, and inflamed;
For it gives her power to rebuild the man's soul and release his pain.

The core of a lady's elegance is seldom seen by the naked eye;
But it is through this sight that her urbanity begins to multiply.

A lady's elegance is something she did not create;
She was destined to be by the ONE who chose her fate.

A lady's elegance is not something to be destroyed;
It is to be nutured, cherished, and enjoyed.

A lady's elegance is hailed as precious and true;
Yes, a lady's elegance is the epitome of you.

LUST

The lust for your love yearns deep in my veins,
That burning sensation will likely remain.

Once cool and in control, these feelings could not be manipulated;
But now, these feelings are self activated.

I must admit that these feelings are genuine when they escape;
Perhaps it's better that way, for through you they originate.

My lust for you will never, never, never end;
You keep me hungry for you again and again.

SUSPENDED OBSESSION

Upon our first touch the message was quite clear;
Of us being parallel someday, oh I hope that day is near.

The softness of your body and roundness of your hips;
Sweats while in my hands as I kiss your luscious lips.

You are so beautiful and oh so wise;
Later one night I'll caress your tummy and then your thighs.

I want to take you up to the skies to soar;
And be able to penetrate your chastity forever more.

My respect and desire for you are so intimate and intense;
I often forget other thoughts before me, again escapes my common
    sense.

I take deep breaths to savor each moment in time;
Oh, I'm in such awe when you walk away, I stare at your behind.

You keep me from going crazy as I anticipate my thrill;
Cause you put matters in perspective and say, not now; chill!

I WISH I WERE IN PHILLY

I wish I were in Philly with my love so true;
I wish I were in Philly to give my love to you.

I wish I were in Philly to enjoy the arts;
I wish I were in Philly for you surely warm my heart.

I wish I were in Philly to listen to the symphony;
I wish I were in Philly because you are the one meant for me.

I wish I were in Philly to make a final bet;
I wish I were in Philly to prove I could have you yet.

I wish I were in Philly, but able to dodge the pollution;
I wish I were in Philly to submerge in our exotic solution.

I wish I were in Philly to spend my final days;
I wish I were in Philly with you forever, to reap your tender ways.

Yes, I wish I were in Philly, holding you so tight;
For being with you in Philly would be my heart's delight.

FIRST AND FOREMOST

I had never been in love before, then I met you;
Now that I am in love, I don't know what else to do.

I often sit and speculate how life would be;
If I had you for myself, for the whole world to see.

What does love mean? I often sit and wonder;
It overpowers you like a river's current, before it takes you under.

Love is seeing your face in my mind, when you are not here;
It's an easy task for me, making your image appear.

So, during unhappy hours, I'm poised to erase;
Those depressing thoughts that linger, til I recreate your face.

You deserve much more from life, I want to pay your account;
The price is insignificant, regardless of the amount.

You have not really lived until you find your own true love;
You can spot her immediately, she's simply a cut above.

How you obtain her is fun, frustrating, and complicated;
She could have desires of her own, and you were never anticipated.

Make your thoughts known to her about your desires and lust;
For she has the right to know, before your gonads bust.

I wrote this poem to express and release the inner me;
So you could understand the fire inside and how it burns for thee.

WHO IS THAT LADY

I know this lady for which I have a burning desire;
I hope to make love to her before I expire.

I know this lady who is quite classy and chic;
She wears elegant clothes every day of the week.

I know this lady who has the key to my heart's chamber;
Some day I hope she notices me, but if not, I won't blame her.

I know this lady who is featured in my dreams;
For there she hosts me, we really work as a team.

Yes, I know this lady through and through;
But all I really need to know is that she longs for me too.

TELL IT LIKE IT IS

Do not resist your heart for it is right;
Do not resist the love we give each other tonight.

Do not regret those experiences you had before;
For there will come a time for reflection once more.

Dream those dreams that motivate your spirit to bloom;
Let those emotions lead you to me real soon.

The way is being cleared for us to unite;
Then we'll be regarded as a celestial delight.

So that ceremonious ritual of us being one;
Will bring us our destined strength, love, and fun.

Tell it like it is, proclaim it to all you know;
Take your mate with you, now there is someone to show.

THE THOUGHT OF YOU

I've only known you for a short time
But when we first met I knew then, you would be mine.

Perhaps we plan how things should occur;
Or we just focus on what we prefer.

What's so special about our fate
Is that it's inevitable that we will mate.

Lets go dancing into the night so I can give you a twirl;
We'll come home tired and exhausted, but I will still rock your world.

Life deals you a hand to win, loose, or draw;
That is great for me because, I can't wait to get under your bra.

As I close my thoughts, please remember this;
I truly, truly, enjoy the thrill of your kiss.

I will see you tonight, again, in my dreams;
As I fall asleep knowing we became a team.

MY MADONNA LILY

The Madonna Lily is an elegant flower;
One gazes at her beauty hour after hour.

For her splendor and charm engulf your mind;
Listen to your heartbeat as you reminisce intimate times.

When you gather her flower to highlight your bouquet;
She brings much joy and fulfillment and brightens your day.

Some say the Madonna Lily only blossoms in spring;
My dearest blooms forever, just listen to my heart sing.

Your Madonna Lily will bloom for you if your heart is true;
Her beautiful flower is the symbol of her love for you.

My Madonna Lily will stay with me through all time;
It's nice to have a flower in your life, you are mine.

WHAT A WEEK

I fell in love on Monday; by Tuesday it was still going strong;
Wednesday she was sexier and sweeter, on Thursday we danced the
   whole night- long.

On Friday she brought me breakfast in bed, when Saturday rolled
   around there was more pounding in my heart.
On Sunday we took a walk in the park, we had a picnic lunch on our
   blanket and kissed until way after dark.

I know I love this lady, she is so special to me;
I hope to be with her forever and that she will marry me.

If I told you how we met you would not believe my luck;
I saw her on the road, stranded, while driving my truck.
And now, even I believe in good luck.

Vern Alford

CLARICE, MY SWEET

Clarice my sweet, with eyes so true and beautifully brown;
I gleam with joy when they look at me, they seem to want me around.

Clarice my sweet, why I beckoned your way during this season?
It's a phenomenon to me, true love often comes without obvious
    reason.

Clarice my sweet, afar my life was incomplete and, oh, so bland;
But when you appeared on the scene, then life seemed so grand.

Clarice my sweet, oh where do we go from here?
Lets go in unison, even if destined beyond this hemisphere.

Clarice my sweet, we have been soulmates for many moons;
We'll join together in our earthly celebration, creating another real
    soon.

Clarice my sweet, how hollow we were before our first embrace;
But now our hearts are full, and emptiness, there's no trace.

Clarice my sweet, each night before I lay down to rest;
I praise GOD for you, HE has given me the best.

Clarice my sweet, wherever you roam, if by chance we are apart;
You'll know life's true meaning for us, and Baby, you really stole my
    heart.

A TOUCH OF SUNSHINE

A touch of sunshine with all its radiant glow;
A touch of sunshine, warms me so.

A touch of sunshine is what I want to see;
A touch of sunshine is you looking at me.

A touch of sunshine is captured in your every smile;
A touch of sunshine is always guilty when put on trial.

A touch of sunshine travels to distant land;
A touch of sunshine from you landed on this lucky man.

A touch of sunshine is a pleasant attribute to have;
A touch of sunshine has happiness as a pal.

A touch of sunshine is here in every season;
A touch of sunshine appears, unrequested, and without reason.

A touch of sunshine travels lightning fast;
A touch of sunshine on you, lasts, and lasts, and lasts.

A touch of sunshine knows what I must do;
A touch of sunshine told me to admit, "I LOVE YOU".

YOU DON'T NEED MAKEUP

You don't need makeup, this you might not know;
You don't need makeup, just let your beauty show.

You don't need makeup, don't cover up your face;
You don't need makeup, your lovliness can't be replaced.

You don't need makeup, there is no need, you see;
You don't need makeup, there is none as fine as thee.

You don't need makeup, there is nothing you need to improve;
You don't need makeup, your face is already baby smooth.

You don't need makeup, find other ways to spend your time;
You don't need makeup, you are already so damn fine.

You don't need makeup, check yourself out in the mirror;
You don't need makeup, your skin is already smooth, none clearer.

You don't need makeup, take a trip and have some fun;
You don't need makeup, you're already the prettiest under the sun.

You don't need makeup, you are fine just the way you are;
You don't need makeup, put those cosmetics back in the jar.

You don't need makeup, my eyes know the truth;
You don't need makeup, you are already the fountain of youth.

You don't need makeup, your beauty is already revealed;
You don't need makeup, you can never be consealed.

You don't need makeup, there is nothing else to say;
You don't need makeup, go ahead and call it a day.

You don't need makeup, your daughters are blessed;
They won't need makeup either, you already took and aced the test.

A LEG MAN

I'm a leg man, I like women's legs, all kinds;
Legs support the sexiest foundation you'll ever find.

I like black legs that support my favorite crew;
Your legs are sexy and only worthy of you.

I like white legs, they walk with grace and style;
They are so cute and fine, they really make me smile.

I like tan legs, they are so unique;
I want to wrestle them under the satin sheets.

I like red legs, they get your attention, too;
These legs are fiesty, no telling what they might do.

I like brown legs, seen on many people of the world;
I like them when they dance, giving the body a twirl.

I like yellow legs found on the sophisticated crew;
You have georgous legs, they look great on you.

I like big legs, long legs, short legs, skinny legs and all;
They support all those sexy ladies and make sure they don't fall.

I like sturdy legs underneath a pair of jeans, every now and then;
I like those classy legs best, they might need a friend.

Yes, I'm a leg man and proud to be;
Many women strut their stuff just for me to see.

If there are any legs out there I failed to mention;
You are in a class alone, you get special attention.

You guys who aren't leg men, I don't know what to say;
Remember, legs are what bring all the sexy ladies your way.

Vern Alford

HIGH MAINTENANCE WOMAN

I have a high maintenance woman, I am such a lucky man;
All the guys envy me, my woman lets me have all I can.

Everyday if I want it, there is no excuse;
She says, go ahead knock yourself out, put that tool to good use.

Monday through Friday and on the weekend too;
My woman wants so much maintenance, and gets it, that's true.

I ask her for the "honey do list", when I have time;
Number one on her list, "maintain me, right now is fine".

A man does not have many basic drives and that's at the top of his
list;
My lady frequently asks me to maintain her, that she insists.

A high maintenance woman, with that great appetite;
Will find another maintenance man if you don't have the might.

Still, get the high maintenance woman if you got the drive;
She'll keep you motivated, she'll definitely keep you alive.

My high maintenance woman has all she can take;
Guys, make sure you do this too, for your own sake.

All you high maintenance women out there, you know who you are;
If you have the right maintenance man, he'll never look afar.

Some other women, refer to high maintenance women, as someone
bad;
But she wants a mate like that for herself, to keep her from going
mad.

Guys, before you settle on a mate, make sure she is high maintenance, too;

For then you'll have a life full of happiness, maintenance, and pleasure for you.

THE PLEASING PRINCESS

Not a prince, but had much fun as a kid;
Stumbling upon a princess was actually what I did.

The right place during a school tour;
I fancied a princess to try to lure.

Her oil baron Dad hosted a school function;
Not knowing I wanted his daughter's petticoat junction.

The pool party, where I caught her eye;
She purposefully walked by just to say hi.

Dropped a note behind a bush for me;
Telling me to meet her by the pussy willow tree.

Over there we made our secret plan to play;
I would climb up to her room at the end of the day.

Waiting for nightfall took forever and a day;
I wanted the princess, she seemed to feel the same way.

Once inside her room there was nothing to say;
We had waited forever, now we wanted to play.

Not a thing on as she laid wanting on her bed;
I anxiously walked over to her and she said, go ahead.

Moments of ecstasy passed as we took our trip;
I held her close, firmly grasping her petite hips.

Therapy was over, what a great session;
She said, "Come again, anytime, for another lesson".

Her Mom called, I closely escaped being seen;
That was the last I saw of the princess, we were a brief team.

Seeing oil today puts memories in my mind;
About being with the princess, having a good ole time.

Vern Alford

INTENSITY

I never knew intensity until I held your hand,
Your energy jolted me more than I thought I would understand.

I never knew intensity until I looked into your eyes,
Lying deep inside was the love I soon realized.

I never knew intensity until that first deep kiss,
Something suddenly overwhelmed me, something I can't resist.

I never knew intensity until I first heard you call my name,
I had heard others call it before, but it didn't sound quite the same.

I never knew intensity until our first embrace,
I was truly mesmerized, I want to forever be in your embrace.

I never knew intensity until our relationship started,
But I know intensity now, never again to be broken hearted.

TEA BAGGING TINA

Tea bagging Tina, in a class all by herself;
Can teabag any guy better than anybody else.

She got me hipped, I had no clue;
She made a man out of me, this can happen to you.

Once believed experienced, I was in doubt;
But she put something on me I never dreamed about.

I can't explain the technique, but this you must know;
Once she gets a hold of you, you hope she will never let go.

Tea bagging Tina deserves a Ph.D., that's the truth;
She'll give you the thrill of a lifetime, to that I am proof.

Guys, if you have never been tea bagged before, that's too bad;
But once you get it, you'll definitely know you have been had.

It's a work of art, a craft that keeps you in suspense;
Those who mastered the technique will make you lose your sense.

Tea bagging Tina, you, I'll always remember;
From January of every year, through December.

WHAT A BREEZE

On break during a filming scene;
Would produce the most popular picture ever seen.

A picture then so unique, destined to change time;
You see many look alikes now, but none as graceful or fine.

The camera was still on, who knew;
That it would frame a picture to thrill us too.

That full dress blowing in the wind;
Gave us guys a vision we'll see again and again.

An unlikely place to be standing that day;
On top of the vent, over the New York subway.

The train passed swiftly, releasing such a strong breeze;
That those who saw the scene fell to their knees.

The fantasy was fulfilled for those who saw;
From their faces was coined the phrase, "Pick Up Your Jaw".

What a rare find during those days;
For it would start its own fashion parade.

If by now you still have no clue;
I'll give a little hint, just for you.

Then the most photographed scene known to man;
From that moment could be held in anybody's hand.

I'm talking about Norma Jean, aka, Marilyn Monore;
She is the star in this popular picture show.

SHE DRESSES HER MAN

She buys me stylish ties to wear around my neck;
These ties are fashionable and trendy, yet she keeps me in check.

She observes my physique to determine my gear;
Others notice my fashion, but women know her hand is near.

I often complain that she spends too much time;
But she is quick to remind me, I'm hers, I will dress fine.

Secretly, I long for her tedious and tender care;
For others comment on my apparel, I get noticed everywhere.

She watches over me wherever I go;
She wants to know I'm spoken for, this does show.

I truly cherish this woman who loves me indeed;
She has high aspirations for me, and dresses me to succeed.

The success of a man can be measured by his woman's quest,
So a man should observe how his woman insists he dresses.

So tonight I rest comfortably in my bed;
For tomorrow she'll dress me sharp from my feet to my head.

Oh I love what she does, I don't want to appear mean;
But I feel best in a T-shirt and an old pair of jeans.

HAPPY BIRTHDAY

Happy birthday sweet baby, to the one I truly love;
You have been an inspiration to me, you're simply a cut above.

Happy birthday sweet baby, today is suited for you;
So I want to bring joy to your heart and be your fantasy too.

Happy birthday sweet baby, it has such a pleasant sound;
For once our hearts were searching, today they are found.

Happy birthday sweet baby, how can I ever express?
All the joy you brought into my life, filling it with happiness.

Happy birthday sweet baby, may you forever be blessed;
For what you have touched has no more emptiness.

Happy birthday sweey baby, I truly hope you enjoyed today;
For it is fitting for you to have things your own special way.

Happy birthday sweet baby, and I wish you many more;
I hope to be part of your life forever, to love, cherish, and adore.

HANDYMAN JAKE

Glad it's Friday, can't wait to get home;
Have myself a bubble bath, but will be all alone.

It's my time to rejuvenate, relax and reflect;
I do this often, for me I do not neglect.

Turned on the faucet, the water gushed out rusty and brown;
What handyman could I call who lived on this side of town?

Oh yes, handyman Jake, lives just over the ridge;
He's reasonable, doesn't charge much, I have beer in the frig.

Quickly I ran to get my cell;
This was an emergency for me, what a living hell.

The knob on the faucet broke, water everywhere;
Thought I would be swimming by the time someone got there.

Be there in a flash Miss Becky, hang on and stay calm;
Soon he pounded on the door and I jumped into his arms.

Jake, there is water everywhere, this place is a mess;
Let me find the shut-off value, it's over there, I guess.

As Jake began to trouble shoot, I cleaned up as much as I could;
Miss Becky, it's your water filter, it's clogged and no good.

I have one in my truck, I'll get a new faucet too;
Then I'll reconnect everything, all will be as good as new.

Everything is working fine now, Jake is a life saver;
Then I did something very strange for my behavior.

Jake, order us a pizza delivery, my treat, I'll get a quick shower;
Not knowing I was that long, I returned in about an hour.

The pizza was there, sliced and on the table set for two;
He was just sitting there and said I waited for you.

As we began to eat he asked how had I been;
Fine, but this old house is nickeling and diming me again.

I'll check some things out before I leave, you'll be all right;
As Jake returned I handed him a beer and said all I have is light.

We talked for awhile, he was very sensitive and calm;
I was shaking and very tense, he stroked and grabbed my arm.

As he stood, he gave me a shoulder massage, it was right on time;
I just thought to myself, I wish this guy was mine.

Miss Becky, I've got to go, I don't mean to impose;
You can stay if you like, I know you have a good soul.

If you must go, do one more thing for me, if you will;
Install my mirror, its leaning on my bedroom window sill.

Mount it on the closet door, just a little beyond my height;
I need it to get dressed, to make sure things are alright.

You always look great, Miss Becky, you are the bomb;
You'll make someone a good wife and definitely be a great mom.

She went over to the mirror, examined it and did her hair;
Suddenly her robe fell off, she just stood there.

Such an amazing body from head to feet;
He picked her up, took her to bed, laid her on the sheet.

Looking me square in the eyes, what are you going to do?
Just relax, Miss Becky, I'm going to make love to you.

The smell of bacon and eggs helped to get Jake awake;
She said wake up sleepy head, it's time you ate.

You are a good handyman Jake, you really know what to do;
Consider being my handyman, you'll get benefits too.

Ladies, choose a handyman, in case things do break;
He'll be able to fix it, then your vanity he'll take.

DOWN, NOT OUT

Went to work early this morning, I was eager you know.
My boss came by and said, "I' m sorry, I got to let you go".

I packed my stuff and went to a bar to think;
I sat there at least 45 minutes, looking at that same ole drink.

At the other end of the bar sat an attractive and classy lady;
She looked poised and chic, she didn't look shady.

As she walked by, her scarf landed on a seat next to mine;
I retrieved it for her and she gave me the oddest line.

Follow me, don't say a damn word or I'll change my mind;
Follow her indeed, I was curious and didn't waste any time.

A short cab ride to the Uptown Holiday Inn;
I just did as she said, but had a sheepish grin.

In her room she asked, "What is your story, man?
Baby, I had a bad day, I just got canned.

Talk no more, it's your lucky day and I'll cheer you up real nice;
I said to myself, you don't have to tell me twice.

We got busy, very busy doing the do, you know;
She said, I'm glad you stopped by that bar, man you can really go.

The woman was georgous and stacked real good;
She put some loving on me only a horny woman could.

Hours passed, from exhaustion we feel into a deep sleep;
Later, when I did awake, all I saw on the bed were sheets.

The lady was gone, but left her card and a hand written note;
I was pleasantly surprised after reading what she wrote.

Call me sometime if you liked what you had and saw;
Her business card read, Linda Bishop, Attorney at Law.

I just might know of a job, you can certainly do;
And along with that, you'll get fringe benefits, too.

Fellows, if you ever lose your job, don't lose your cool, too;
Be patient, a gig like this just might become available to you.

HE'LL NEVER CHEAT

Ladies are always wondering whether their men will ever cheat;
I say, take action with your thang, keep him between the sheets.

Men are very visual, they like things to see;
Put that stuff right in his face, put it where he'll be.

Wear him out when he gets you, keep begging for more;
Tell him he's powerful, tell him he is outta sight for sure.

Shine his pipe, keep it nice and straight and grab ahold;
Do him justice when you service it, he'll lose his control.

If he passes out leave him alone, just let him be;
Because when he gets awake he'll remember his fantasy.

As he gets out of bed make sure he smells his favorite food;
That will get him ready again, really put him in the mood.

Deny him then, say you need your strength so you'll be strong;
Cause when you finish your meal, you'll keep you in me all day long.

As he eats, grab his pipe and pump it real fast;
Look him dead in his eyes, see how long he'll last.

As he wants to explode, pump it real hard until he says ouch;
Quickly run away and doggie style your nude self across the couch.

When he leaps towards you, arch your back and purr like a cat in
    heat;
He'll soon be deep inside you, giving you a powerful treat.

Keep this cycle going everyday, if you can;
He'll soon discover that he is a lover man.

He'll ask how he did, here is what you say right then;
Just say, Baby, you are damn awesome, lets do it again.

Men won't go looking when his woman is off the chain;
He'll be content to stay at home, thats where he'll remain.

MARRIED, BUT

Happily married suburban housewife, not a care in life;
Thought she was contented with her lifestyle, being a housewife.

Just her usual noon bridge game with the girls around the block;
She was always home by four for sure, she watched the clock.

The game ended early, the ladies went out for a drink;
A distinguished guy at the end of the bar gave her a wink;

Paid him no mind, he was of no interest to her, you see;
He soon left, she thought good, I'm glad he let me be.

Later, the girls began to leave, each going their own separate way;
Standing by her car was that guy from the bar, he had something to say.

Ma'am, I don't mean to impose, but inside you weren't enjoying
    yourself.
You are definitely an attractive and classy lady, you are top shelf.

I'm not your husband, but he is a fool I'd say;
Allowing you to be unhappy and unfulfilled all day.

I beg your pardon, you are certainly out of line;
My husband and I are in love, we are doing just fine.

Why you talking to me, a stranger you don't even know?
Sorry I wasted your time, now get in your car and go.

He seemed so upset, being a woman she had to inquire;
Was shocked when he said, rich ladies just want to be admired.

Oh no, you got me all wrong, for me there is more to life;
Maybe thats true, but you're not happy only being his wife.

Why do you say that, me you don't even know?
But with the right offer from me, you'll gladly go.

Lovely lady, I'm staying at the Holiday Inn on Elm Street, room 208;
You can meet me there if you dare, unless I made a mistake.

So damn angry, she left in a rush, firmly gripping the wheel, speeding
    away;
But some how ended up on Elm Street, with him she wanted to play.

Once in his room, he kissed her passionately and so long;
She almost fell to her knees, but his embrace was very strong.

With a slight of hand, her clothes were off and on the floor;
He laid her on the bed, hit pay dirt and began to score.

The game was not tied, the score not even close;
She went into ecstasy very often, but he scored the most.

To her those Wednesday bridge games are now unappealing;
She mostly sits there and stare, they don't know what she is feeling.

Ladies, housewives, you got to live a little, life can be too routine;
Unless you encounter someone special, you'll never know what that
    means.

WINE AND DINE HER

Wine and dine her, not just a tale you heard;
She'll know your intent, you'll get what you deserve.
Wine and dine her, not just a tale you heard;
She'll know your intent, you'll get what you deserve.

Here is a basic rule of how guys must behave;
One thing you must get right, its like learning how to shave.

Women are observant, not just verbal, they don't miss a trick;
If you come at them wrong, another man she might pick.

Never speak of your intent or rush into the groove;
Most guys don't play it right, they make too quick of a move.

She has her own inner clock, you'll know when it's twelve;
She'll give you clues, just listen, you'll be able to tell.

Wine and dine her, not just a tale you heard;
She'll know your intent, you'll get what you deserve.
Wine and dine her, not just a tale you heard;
She'll know your intent, you'll get what you deserve.

The art of making love is a ritual, too often not done right;
If you follow these basic rules everything will be outta sight.

Timing is everything, never watch the clock;
She'll then believe you're impatient and put you on lock.

Be decisive, take charge and always present a gift;
For if you later stumble, you won't fall off the cliff.

As she makes her decision about whether you two will mate;
Again be patient, unless she insists you not wait.

Wine and dine her, not just a tale you heard;
She'll know your intent, you'll get what you deserve.
Wine and dine her, not just a tale you heard;
She'll know your intent, you'll get what you deserve.

As you close the deal, still play with her deck;
Take nothing for granted or she'll put you in check.

You'll surely know if you did your job well;
Her toes will curl and there might be a yell.

Thank her for her gift to you, she'll want you to be polite;
Another encounter could happen in the future or later that same
    night.

Never tell a soul of your experience, it just ain't right;
For if she wants others to know, it should be her delight.

Wine and dine her, not just a tale you heard;
She'll know your intent, you'll get what you deserve.
Wine and dine her, not just a tale you heard;
She'll know your intent, you'll get what you deserve.

Part Three:
Recognition, Advice
And A Twist

I WEAR SHADES

I wear shades to protect my eyes from the sun's glare;
The lenses filter the rays which seem to come from everywhere.

I wear shades so my eyes can roam openly and free;
Very often they look at people who are looking back at me.

I wear shades because they look very cool, boss and sharp;
Besides, why strain your eyes and be unable to navigate in the dark.

I wear shades, they come in many colors, some look fly;
I suggest you have more than one pair, not just one to rely.

I wear shades during the summer, winter, spring and fall;
Wearing shades all year is actually no bother at all.

I wear shades everywhere, they are a part of me;
I fashion my gear so my shades aren't the only thing you see.

I come from a long line of shade wearers, it is a tradition for us;
We wear shades all the time, for us it's a must.

You should wear shades too, just try them and observe;
All those things you'll see, now you're ahead of the curve.

Pick your shades carefully, not just any ole pair will do;
Cause what you wear on your face is a reflection of you.

I SALUTE YOU

You work hard each day providing for troubled youth;
You give them hope, show them dignity, and tell them the truth.

Most can't do your job because it's so unique;
You are sometimes criticized, but you always land on your feet.

I admire what you have accomplished in just a few years;
For many believed it impossible, but you really perservered.

So it's fitting that we honor you for all your many skills;
And let these small tokens be gestures of our good will.

REALITY

Traveling across this vast land I see
That there is a suitable place for me.

Driving various routes towards my destination;
Hardly allowed much time to enjoy my vacation.

I once believed the big lie told about this place;
That it's so populated we'll soon run out of space.

One is often told things that are not real;
Unfortunately, those tales lure you with their appeal.

Sometimes you realize the truth in life;
Try to know it before the ultimate sacrifice.

NOT APPRECIATED

On my job, I often and without prodding do
Those things which are taxing that nobody else knows how or wants
to.

I research, organize, schedule, listen, and arrange;
Projects for my boss that would actually drive him insane.

People tend to seek my opinion on matters that count;
Amazingly, I give them information in significant amount.

Why I continue to perform these feats without compensation or
adortion
Is but a mystery because I know I deserve more appreciation.

Those of us who perform our jobs well, do it with flair
Should not worry about replacement because none could compare.

God gave me great talent, desire, and skill
Which I gladly use to help fulfill His will.

I feel better now since being described as unique;
I will surely feel better tomorrow as I strut my new physique.

SECRETARY'S DAY

On this day I give you praise;
For being so special in so many ways.

I would lose my head if it wasn't for you;
For guidance on the job, I come to you, too.

I act important and try to give orders;
You act responsible and remind me of my borders.

How you get all that work done, I have no idea;
But I do know that without you, nothing seems clear.

You run the office with skill and class;
I watch your techniques with awe for I know they can't be surpassed.

Your job is tough, but you do it with such flair;
You handle complaints to my office and are always fair.

So, I honor you today and throughout this week;
For your dedication and tenaciousness, these are never ending feats.

I'M ON VACATION

I'm on vacation, I'm having fun;
I'm on vacation, riding into the sun.

I'm on vacation, no hassles to ponder
I'm on vacation, looking out onto the wide blue wonder.

I'm on vacation, now I can be free;
I'm on vacation, and will truly act like me.

I'm on vacation, where I'll get my rest;
I'm on vacation, so I will get things off my chest.

I'm on vacation, this time is reserved;
I'm on vacation, now nothing gets on my nerves.

I'm on vacation, for I have earned this time;
To just sit down, relax, enjoy you, and have a glass of bubbly wine.

ALLERGIC

When it comes to getting sick I'm quite immune;
But I can't stand to be around ragweed, pollen, or certain perfume.

I've been brave and strong throughout all these years;
Until pollen, ragweed, or some perfume fill my eyes with tears.

Talking and joking for me is something I do with ease;
But at times I rush my words to ready this body for the approaching
sneeze.

When you're allergic to certain items that are so routine;
You quickly learn to compensate so your sneeze does not create a
scene.

I've learned throughout the years that systems do break down, then
need repair;
Yes, I've learned to maintain and monitor my system so its not in
despair.

Allergies are just nature's way to remind our bodies of its peak;
For then one must replenish those electrolytes so the body is not too
weak.

Do not ignore nature's warning, especially if it's fast;
Just take note, make adjustments, and those symptoms should pass.

ONCE A NERD - BUT NOW

Nerds, I once believed, were people known as square;
Now, to my surprise, people seek nerds who are seldom shunned
anywhere.

How they got a bad reputation, perplexes me, even still today;
For I always envied nerds who performed unique tasks in their own
special way.

The computer age made nerds popular and respected;
But I remember, back in the day, when we all made sure they were
rejected.

Nerds have quickly distinguished themselves through high technology;
Now as we come across nerds we've harassed, we are quick with the
apology.

Our laughter and joking about nerds was once a popular scheme;
Many of these nerds got the last laugh, they reached success beyond
our wildest dream.

I sat next to a nerd in class, she said I was a pest;
But during mid-terms I was cozy with her until I passed the test.

So, think back on those nerds of yesterday and where they are now;
For many of them are in the limelight now, quick to take a bow.

I often think of my own nerdiness when I was a child;
Many of those nerdy ideas now actually make matters worthwhile.

WATER ON THE ROCKS

Water on the rocks refreshes and quenches your thirst;
I've had better tasting drinks before, but I choose water first.

It leaves no residue nor aftertaste to entice your sences;
But it is sure to fulfill its duty and your thirst it really quenches.

Much of it is polluted now, so cherish each and every drop;
Get on board to challenge those whose pollution has to stop.

Whether you drink other liquids is something you can decide;
But the precious drink of water is required to keep you alive.

Many of us take for granted that it will always be here;
But in what form it will remain is definitely not clear.

When you see and think of water and all the beauty it brings;
Remember, protect this vital resource that's necessary for all living
    things.

Vern Alford

THE PIRATE'S CAUSE

Pirates and thieves once roamed the open seas;
They wreaked havoc on the innocent and brought navies to their knees;

Their place in history is often disputed;
But their gorey lifestyle was often reputed.

Hired by many to achieve a basic mission;
They pursued their own goals, what a crafty position.

There are still some pirates today who influence our lives;
We don't readily recognize them in their clever disguise.

Whose mission they are performing now, is not always clear;
But there is evidence of them still lurking throughout this hemisphere.

So, as you witness situations going from bad to extreme;
Here is a friendly reminder, pirates are still on the scene.

SEIZE THE MOMENT

I had a thought the other day, but did not write it down;
I had a fence to mend, but instead I went to town.

I had a dollar just a while ago, I could not wait to spend;
Perhaps I use money too rapidly and hope it will reappear again.

I had this feeling yesterday of you, but didn't get the chance to tell;
How great and wonderful you are, for you are so swell.

I looked around for those things I had yesterday, but now they are
    lost;
Today I'll gladly buy those things, almost at any cost.

Tomorrow if things come to me, I'll be quick to react;
For I do not like eating my words or having to back track.

Vern Alford

FOOD FOR THOUGHT

Black-eyed peas, chicken, rice and greens;
Are the dishes I had to eat as a teen.

Those foods kept me sharp and fit;
But now I favor those foods that make me sick.

You see, cheese, wheat, and too much red meat;
Actually clog your arteries and make them weak.

I strived to be successful so I could eat;
Caviar, pizza, and other special treats.

But eating those rich foods, too many to mention;
Has strained my heart with hypertension.

Being greedy I was too stubborn to tell;
That those basic foods actually kept me well.

Now we spend our time with the medicine man;
Who tell us to eat the basic foods bland.

The grass seems greener on the other side of the street;
So throughout your life journey, be careful what you eat.

THE ERECTION

Got to tell this story, some might initially find too bold;
It's not really that bad, but something that needed to be told.

I remember when it first happened, what a great day;
The surprise of my lifetime, at that moment, and I wanted it to stay.

Dad had always told me, what goes up will come down;
Hoping he was wrong, I wanted it to forever hang around.

Let me tell you how it happened, check out this detail;
I had tried many things before, but many of them failed.

A skinny little kid then, now maybe a surprise to many;
But what I was about to do, nobody would believe, not any.

I was getting the urge to get things started and spring into action;
But knew I had to find a private place, to avoid others' reaction.

Everything was in place, I closely checked my equipment to be sure;
For I was about to do something very revealing, I had to be mature.

Completing the foundation was not an easy task;
But that needed to be done or the erection would not last..

I followed all instructions and surprisingly things sprang into place;
After it was completed, a real big grin was on my face.

For it was my 7th birthday and I wanted to impress;
I couldn't wait to show my family my results, this was my best.

I exited my room with the erection in my hands;
So proud of myself, I just stood there like a man.

Dad saw it first, gave me a distinctive stare;
Then there was Mom, hers was a lasting glare.

Shocked at their reaction, I didn't know what to do;
Both then laughed, saying, we are so proud of you.

You did it all by yourself, never asking for a hand;
Now that you have done that, you are certainly a man.

I loved that Lincoln Log Set, it was the greatest present for a boy;
Putting that set together, much better than playing with a dumb ole
    toy.

Erecting that Lincoln Log (lego) Set was definitely a work of art;
I always knew it would be great, even before the start.

The thrill was over, so I put the Set away;
Knowing I could duplicate that erection, anyday.

YOUR ASSETS

The cost of love is a price I'm willing to pay;
An investment in you, yielding dividends each and everyday.

Protect your assets, that's what people say;
I'll guard our account so others stay away.

I put us first as we plan our goals;
We have made great moves, many very bold.

I get my payoff daily without any reminder;
You are so special to me, there is none kinder.

So if you have an investment you're planning to make;
Choose your options carefully, don't make a mistake.

Life long earnings are commodities we produce;
Our portfolio is complete now, it is surely tamper proof.

Your assets and investments, please cherish throughout all your days;
For that is the core of you, what a foundation you have laid.

EVIL BE GONE

Traces of evil are found throughout this universe;
Don't invest in or look for it, that will make you worse.

Why many choose evil to occupy their life is beyond me;
I will never choose evil over goodness, it just cannot be.

If you ever want to get beyond evil, it's not hard to do;
Just look around and inside and capture the beauty in you.

When you see your goodness, then you'll know;
That those evil things you did in the past, got to go.

When you did evil, you were not bad;
You just happened not to realize all the good fortune you had.

While you are practicing evil it doesn't need to look for you;
For you are a constant customer, it knows what you will do.

In times of transition, evil is on the fence;
That is the best time, to permanently put evil on the bench.

So, if you now come upon evil, look it square in the eye;
Then, your righteous ways will bid evil a forever goodbye.

WHAT A MAN WANTS

A man wants three things in a woman and they must be on time;
He wants a woman to cook, represent, and treat him real fine.

He wants an executive in the Boardroom, who is very confident;
One who skillfully handles all issues and problems she is sent.

As long as she holds it down, no matter the profession;
For what she does will teach others a good lesson.

A chef in the kitchen, who can whip up a fine dish;
That keeps his tummy satisfied, better than he wish.

She needs to be fast, good, and versatile;
So her man, her lover, can feast in style.

A freak in the bedroom is definitely a must, you know;
For he wants her to be the star of the show.

Her desire must be strong and intense to the core;
So when they do the do, she'll always want more.

I tell you these things because men are not complex;
We are very basic creatures who love food, intelligence, and very good
   sex.

When you get the chance, show him these things, he'll never let go of
   you;
The secret to capturing and keeping a good man, lies in what you are
   willing to do.

A MAN IS

A man is bold, strong, and mighty;
A man is poised, cool, and sometimes untidy.

A man is curious, challenging, intense and proud;
A man often hides his emotions, but defends his position and might
be loud.

A man likes things perfect, straight and exact;
A man is so bold that he says and does things he can't take back.

A man is sometimes threatened, but quickly defends his rights;
A man often has internal emotions, but rarely admits that he is
uptight.

A man is brilliant, determined, gutsy and smart;
Most men recognize that women are truly a work of art.

A man is predictable, consistent and rigid;
Some men never acknowledge when it is cold, nippy or frigid.

A man is sometimes tense, uptight and often perturbed;
A man has intimate thoughts to share, but is often too reserved.

Cars, sports, women and male boss bashing men discuss with ease;
Asking men to venture much beyond this, is not such a breeze.

A man is loving, sensitive, caring, and to that there is proof;
But when a man is called to share these feelings, he is generally aloof.

I share these traits about man because I know them to be true;
For I am a man also, I long to be understood by you.

THE O. J. BLUES

The trial of the century is discussed each day;
I really wonder if someone actually framed O. J.

The crime was vicious and beyond what many understand;
I truly wonder whether it was perpetrated by this man.

I do not condone those killings, but consider this thought;
Of showing a brotha a message he should have long been taught.

That going to the big league you inevitably take a risk;
For that group throws hard balls and curves, and seldom miss.

The prosecuters and defenders, with all their might;
Have again divided this nation into the left and the right.

On one hand there is O. J., the cool, calm, and having confidence.
Then there is the detective who might have planted incriminating
    evidence.

The "N" word has resurfaced with all its connotations;
It is sure to cause resentment, anger, and frustration.

Whether O. J. is the assailant against Ron and Nicole is not clear;
But this trial has been a big spectacle of the western hemisphere.

Believing all things are equal, justice should be served,
But when you are not playing with a full deck, look out for the curve.

JUST AN ORDINARY MAN

I like cooking, working hard, and sometimes doing laundry for fun;
It gives me great pleasure performing these tasks, not relying on anyone.

I like poetry, music, and religious meditation to guide my ideas;
Those thoughts actually ease the pain and calm the fears.

I like the sunset, a cool breeze, and a clear starry night;
I have wished upon a shooting star before it disappeared from sight.

I like challenges, such as mountain climbing, difficult tasks where others failed;
I never hope to face the challenge of getting a "dear John" letter in the mail.

I like intelligent and demanding women who pursue their goals;
They are seldom boring, especially when they release their souls.

I like to spoil my woman, she is never in need;
I take good care of her, she is proud of me, indeed.

I like country living, the mighy oak and an ole dusty dirt road;
These are the places where my memories have been sewed.

I like gospel music, jazz, Mozart and a little rock"n" roll;
But each of these does different things to ease my soul.

I like fast cars, they must be black and real clean;
Some of those shorts are the finest ever seen.

I like working with my hands, never behind a boring desk;
That's for those guys who failed the macho physical test.

I like going to the hoops, a little boxing on the side;
Those things keep me in shape, I can defend my pride.

I like frigid temperatures, especially when I sleep at night;
During those times, I emit radiant heat for my lover's delight.

I like telling jokes, to ordinary folk who appear depressed;
For telling tales is a ritual I use to get things off my chest.

I like raising cane, smooth wine, making passionate love;
What I like most is being sanctioned by THE ALMIGHTY, from
    above.

All those things I like are clues to explain my soul;
I realize these desires exist to fit my lover's mold.

Just an ordinary man, nothing special about me;
But I made my woman happier than she thought she would be.

WOMEN SCHOOLED ME

Women are precious, complex, and sensitive, in need of fulfillment and
    pleasure;
They are not content with any hit or miss, they want ecstasy at their
    leisure.

I've tried to understand them, but realized I had no clue;
About what a woman really wants until I was told what to do.

Just follow our lead and be quick to change and try something new;
We want your undivided attention, patience and romance, too.

When you start something, finish it with style, the favor will return to
    you;
Talk to them, tell them your feelings and always be true.

When you get their commitment, it is sound and strong;
There will be no barriers between you, she'll hang on you all night
    long.

They love to touch, their fingers read emotions;
They will know whether they have your true devotion.

As I became more aware of women, I knew I had been wrong;
For they want a man who is sensitive, he does not have to be, just
    strong.

All you macho only guys, you need to check yourself real fast;
For us sensitive too guys will conquer her, and we will last.

Never underestimate her resolve, thats where many made their mistake;
Accept her strength as an extension of yours, then you'll both have
    what it takes.

JAMES MADISON JOHNSON

James Madison Johnson was his legal name;
But, later in life that name would rightfully change.

He was an unattractive child, ugly, if you want the truth;
He later learned to compensate for it throughout his youth.

In school, girls laughed and teased him, with guys he always got into
    a fight.
But, during all this hassel and ridicule, he learned to hold his hands
    right.

Oversized lips and hair, he had none;
Was the main focus for which we made fun.

The guy was smart, he always had different techniques;
But he was very skinny and did not have a good physique.

Off to college he went to finish his education and schooling;
But, he learned much more than books, everybody he was fooling.

I initially became curious about him at our first Frat party;
He would sit alone in a corner and not appear broken hearted.

Many girls rushed over to him, they would all gather around;
They were unusually quiet, many not making a sound.

Each took turns disappearing with him, for just a little while;
As each girl returned from their seclusion, each had the biggest smile.

Now I was very suspicious and had to inquire;
I asked a friend what was going on, don't be a liar.

She said, James Madison Johnson is the best, he is really great;
He finally realized his destiny and for us, sealed his fate.

He does that thing to us right, while most guys can not;
He does it real good, he knows all the key spots.

We girls had to change his name to something that would fit;
He is no longer James Madison Johnson, to us he is "Lickidy Split".

Why Lickidy Split, you might ask, well if you must know;
He does the greatest thing, EVER, he knows where to go.

I never made fun of him again, I saw him in a different light;
For he had mastered a skill, he had it locked up tight.

I pulled his coatail, and said, Yo Lickidy, can I have a word?
I want you to tell me how to do all that stuff I heard.

Lickidy gave me a few pointers, something I never knew;
He said when the girls find out they'll be after you too.

Throughout this experience, we all got a shocking surprise;
That you think you know somebody, but there is another side.

James Madison Johnson, once the butt of many a joke;
Now as Lickidy Split, he is envied and in awe by all us folk.

DISCO GRANNY

Not too old, just a little beyond eighty-two;
Disco Granny was more limber than me or you.

A mixture of Native American, Black and White;
Would talk trash to anyone, she was born with the right.

She walked with a cane, that was only for show;
You would see her chuck it, when it was time to disco.

Her favorite was the disco duck, her namesake;
Moves so smooth and sharp, you would do a double take.

We would stop dancing and all circle around;
To watch the hippest Granny in any town.

She moved with such ease, style and flair;
People talked about her, almost everywhere.

I remember one move I tried to copy, but forgot;
When I saw it later, it was then called the Robot.

Disco Granny could really party with the best;
The golden lady is gone now, she is at rest.

Still some Disco Grannies around, even today;
Most you won't readily recognize, they have their own way.

The Disco Granny of yesterday already sprouted her seed;
Quietly sits in the background, no need now to take the lead.

Vern Alford

RACISM IS NOT DEAD

Racism is not dead, just look around;
Racism is everywhere, it's not hard to be found.

Racism is in the White House and the highest court of the land;
Look at all the policies and rulings, then you'll understand.

Racism is not dead, once believed amongst the poor;
Many of us are wiser now, we aren't deceived anymore.

Racism is not dead, although it drastically changed its attire;
You see suits, skirts on professionals, some even sing in the church
   choir.

Racism is not dead, check out their websites;
Who do you think own most computers, Blacks or Whites.

Many ordinary people aren't racist, they are like me and you;
Working hard everyday, trying to make a living, too.

Racism is not dead, who do you think have the loud voices;
Yes, the rich and powerful who control most resources;

Racism is not dead, it's readying for another assault;
It's out to teach non-whites a lesson they thought, Blacks, were long
   taught.

Racism is not dead, see all the graffitti on the walls;
Symbols are appearing everywhere, authored by the big and small.

Racism is not dead, but it's running scared with fear;
Thats when it's more hostile and its motive is real clear.

Racism is not dead, it has a master plan;
To reconquer this world and be the law of the land.

Africa is an example right before our eyes;
But we can't see beyond the tribal wars and genocide.

Racism is not dead, just check out all the new plush neighborhoods;
Those who are moving there have all the money and precious goods.

Racism is not dead, once believed a monopoly of the poor;
Check out the rich and powerful, they kick down our door.

Racism is not dead, how many examples do you need;
Before you understand its motivation, manifested by greed.

Racism is not dead, it is definitely alive and even more clever;
There might not be as many of them left, but they will never give up,
    never.

Racism is not dead, but it might be taking its last breath;
But don't let that fool you, it will fight vigorously, til its death.

Racism is not dead and where do you stand?
Do something about it, don't leave it in others' hands.

Racism is not dead and that is the plain ole truth;
But there is hope for our future, it is manifested in our youth.

Racism is not dead, the USA is a melting pot;
It has much diversity, but remember, we are all we got.

Racism is is not dead, but let those bigots know;
That their devisive behavior and ideas, really got to go.

Racism is not dead, but it got caught in its own trap;
Taking its eye off the ball, thought we took a nap.

Vern Alford

Racism is not dead, lets send it out of this universe;
For we know being a racist is the greatest curse.

When racism is dead and gone, generations will know;
That triflin affliction that once plagued us, had to go.

Racism is not dead, it changed its name to another ism;
This one is more chic and fashionable, now its called classism.

Changing its name might throw you off, just look at the intent;
When you reflect on whats going on, you'll know what they meant.

THE CONNECTICUT STROLL

From Hartford, New Haven and Stamford I'm told;
All those folk are doing something, called The Connecticut Stroll.

A stylish walk, so chic and man so upbeat;
Others tried to copy it, but weren't quite as neat.

Guys roll straight, but walk with a distinguished dip;
Ladies are classy and poised when walking, modeling their shapely
    hips.

Stepping in style up the street, around the corner to see;
Those fascinated out-of-towners, trying to be like thee.

Cities and neighborhoods throughout this land have their own style
    of walk;
They envy yours in Connecticut, so they just stare and sulk.

Don't alter your stroll Connecticut, or change it one little bit;
You have that stroll down pat, it's a style that won't quit.

Those of you not fron Connecticut, don't fret, life has a plan for you;
So, stop trying to imitate Connecticut's stroll, for that you cannot do.

About the Author

Vern Alford was born in South Carolina. At a young age his family moved to New Jersey and 2 years later to Pennsylvania where he resides today. He would attend at least 9 different schools in 3 different states before graduating High School. His family moved often because of his father's church ministry. Upon graduating High School, he attended Allen University in Columbia, South Carolina and later Columbus College of Art in Columbus, Ohio.

After undergraduate school Vern was employed by The Commonwealth of Pennsylvania for 25 years in various juvenile justice positions. Later, he became Executive Director of a major juvenile treatment facility. While employed by the Commonwealth he obtained his Masters Degree in Human Services from Lincoln University. After retirement from Pennsylvania Government he was employed, as a Warden, by a private prison management company. Because of his work, Vern has traveled and met people throughout the United States. He has made numerous speaking presentations to various organizations. He also taught graduate courses at a Pennsylvania university.

During his life experiences Vern became more aware of people and many of their motivations. He realized that many people were inspirational, romantic, motivated, pleasure seekers, and often times enjoyed the element of surprise. Vern, always fascinated by poetry, especially enjoyed Poe's, Dickinson's, and Hughes' work. His favorite is The Raven by Edgar Allen Poe. He began to write poems over 30 years ago. However, during those early years he did not share his poetry with anyone. Recently, he has recited his poems at coffee houses and taverns in surrounding communities. He has been well received by those audiences. Because of his popularity he decided to publish some of his poems.

Printed in the United States
47537LVS00004B/394

9 781420 884241